JAZZ MIDNIGHT

JAZZ MIDNIGHT

JACK CRIMMINS

ONE BIRD BOOKS
HATCHVILLE, MASS.

Cover photograph: Mae Blackmore,
"Driving," 2012

Frontispiece photograph:
Mae Blackmore,
"Church Marching Band," 2014

Book design: Jim Morgan and Jack Crimmins

ISBN: 979-8-9898147-1-8

One Bird Books
35 Brush Hill Road
Hatchville, MA 02536
www.onebirdbooks.com
onebirdbooks@gmail.com

CONTENTS

JAZZ MIDNIGHT

ENTER THE POEM DREAMING

enter the poem dreaming
get out of town jazz song
the stones I knew always there
walking away quiet trails
empty avenues
I have traveled the river
the paintings changed
from gold to ashes to gold again
alone darkness drift
everywhere a ghost town
this resiliency of earth
your soul a mirror
rough drafts of old poems
scattered by sudden winds

THE RIVER AROUND THE CORNER

she said she was truly
hidden in the trees
do you resonate with the shadows
moving along the wall
is this the fall of America
tell your companions
begin again
Kenneth Patchen is on the outs
naive sensibilities a guy said
in a postmodern world
where language is fractured
the "I" is disregarded or
scattered across the page
the age of trauma
just beyond the time of terror
why don't we "& why not,
buy a goddamn big car"
as Robert Creeley said
here is the shining light of neon
the shattered glass of healing
hippies in the woods
suburban people
dwellers on
the life of the mind
an architecture of decision
'Whispering Pines' The Band sang
I've got you, hold on
bass solo by Paul Chambers
Red Garland on piano

Kenneth Patchen wrote of love
oh well
keep on anyhow
death and the river
around the corner
quarantine distance
solitude residence
then lightning sparks
a grass fire
thunder in the air
evacuations and
stay safe everyone
in the hills at the river
it's going to be a journey
America's in danger
this is still the land of freedom
I've got news for you

AMARGOSA OPERA HOUSE

nowhere to go nothing to become
stone fortitude tree knowledge
I think of the dancer Marta Becket
of Death Valley Junction
who died recently in her nineties
I've said before she painted visions
on the walls of her theater
waiting in the almost dark
knowing everything I know
will be gone so
I make a few poems
to see what's there to see
poems in the world
women who believe
nights and pathways
a lifelong study of dreams
this is the elegance of afternoons
friends in the east and around town
friends scattered parts unknown

WORLDVIEW

steep canyons and ravens
you can wait years
to return to the desert
winds of risk picking up
sand and tiny pebbles near
creosote and wildflowers
here it is a relaxed morning
there's pomegranates ripe
and falling nearby from
Maria-next-door's tree
we're rich with clouds today
after healing rain beyond
fire smoke dangerous air
now we breathe free
say hello to a stranger
a lost acquaintance maybe
from early wilderness days
and in the Mojave your eyes
catch suddenly in reflection
of the southern sun there
where a winter flash flood
passed by carving a new river
tumbling stones worldview

HIDDEN IN KATHMANDU

I called you.
I knew no other names.
Dirt floor hut, way up
in dark cold mountains
far outside of town.
Or sacred cows
wandering city streets.
Crippled beggar children
right there at the airport.
How do we change?
How do we acquire
knowledge? Writing
these bones. And
bodies, wrapped in
shining colors down
the steps to riverside.
Mourners pray before
burning the corpses at
last. A funeral pyre with
golden sun, sky above.
Alive, alive, today.

DRAGONS

I've heard it said there are immortals
in China writing poems as dragons
with claws on bamboo. Long ago,
held you tight through sorrow,
a wood stove fire on Sonoma Mountain.
Back then we could see the true night.
Dusk taught us secrets.

TOM CLARK IN BOLINAS AND BERKELEY

Tom Clark wrote.
Tom Clark wrote "Death is white,"
wrote "Blue is all right."
If you live in Bolinas
you know the coast.
A litany of names of
poets and writers who
lived there and have died.
Gone and gone on.
Say Joanne Kyger, say
Bobbie Louise Hawkins,
say Robert Creeley, say
Jim Carroll. Carroll's
famous song, with its refrain
"Those are the people that died, died."
Sing that. Sing this.
And now Tom Clark, poet
and writer, is killed by a car,
walking across the street in Berkeley.
He lived, there are books,
his "Beyond the Pale " blog.
I didn't know Tom Clark.
Liked his controversial
biography of Charles Olson.
The man loved baseball.
Had Vida Blue in full
left-handed windup
on the cover of his book
"BLUE." Wrote of Roberto

Clemente, Orlando Cepeda,
a kid in the grandstands
crying because his father
wasn't Reggie Jackson.
"If my father was Reggie
Jackson I could have
anything I want."
I don't love baseball as much
anymore and it surprises
me. I played, all through
high school, led off, played
center, also a lefty,
hit .304 senior year, a few triples,
with a lot of walks. Man, my
on base percentage would have
been stellar if they'd kept
those stats then. Fortunate
to get honorable mention
all-league, a coach said. Okay.
I gave away my glove at forty,
had carried it across the country and back
and mostly don't know the players now.
Still like to think about the history
of baseball and the great names
of the game. Poet Jack Hirschman
claims he was at the game when
Lou Gehrig announced his retirement.
Ill, they named the disease
after him. Lou, The Iron Horse,
saying "Today, I consider
myself the luckiest

man in the world."
This is a poem for Tom Clark.
In Bolinas and Berkeley and
far away he is one of
the west coast greats.
Even though my love for
baseball has faded a bit,
(though, hey, if I was rich
I'd live in North Beach and
have season tickets
to the Giants games and
I'd be back!) I still
watch the World Series, and
any man who writes a book
with Vida Blue in full windup
on the cover is cool by me.
This is a poem for Tom Clark
and for Berkeley and Bolinas.
This is a poem for baseball
and poetry and all the love
in this dangerous world.

SAN FRANCISCO NOW

drive over the Golden Gate
water everywhere then
19th to Cabrillo left on
15th to Fulton left then
right on Stanyan stay
left to turn on Oak
right on Clayton up a couple
blocks to Haight Street very
different scenes early morning
weekday quiet room to move
or crowded tough to park on
weekends all sorts of folks
city dwellers street people
still flowers and tie dye
here we are in some late days
Ginsberg and Kesey quotes
in windows travelers all of us
no big reveal in this City life yet
wake with forest song in mind
abstract intellectualism scatter
words all over as in experiment
poetry as us and them "either/or"
my anthropologist colleague
Ginnie Hine always would say
it's "both/and" meaning inclusive
in poetry or on Haight Street everyone
has a way or place to be sidewalk
crowded or spacious here just here

THE FORGOTTEN POEMS

Some poems last
for a moment, briefly,
before tucked away
in drawers, in boxes,
in the garage on the
invisible *cul de sac*
or stuck in turn around,
to use a movie phrase,
others echo in the mind,
lines reverberating
and many folks have song
as poetry with the great
bands of the sixties
before we knew that
each generation must
find their own music.
The punk bassist Lorna Doom
of the band Germs died
this week and bass player
Mike Watt, initially with
the punk band Minutemen,
when asked what kind of bass
player he was, his friend
D. Boon, the guitarist
for the band, having died in a
van crash thirty years earlier,
said, "I'm D. Boon's bass player."
Jack Gilbert said, it's okay,
if you want to write poems,

you can write poems. Make
your new music in the garage
and put your poems there or
do it like Li Po, famous
Chinese poet, who was said
to write poems on scraps
of paper, then, making
paper boats, floated his
poems downriver along
with the wind.

AT BREW COFFEE HOUSE

all day heat
California blacktop
senses and essences

the way of
mystery birds
distant flyers

another book
of poems
in process

say the woods
are waiting
where has time faded to

if I follow you
up around
Temescal Canyon

breath settles
into rhythm
trust finds a
place

thinking about
fortune and
fate

14

and the great
ocean

days of questions
days of
wild talk

whispering
"turquoise"

think of
bold mountains
once again

how I want you
to know
your life is arriving

now and then
a door opens
bright vision

THE SADNESS AT THE HEART OF
THE NATION

I think of the sadness at the heart
of the nation. Where song fades out.
How there is a train to prison
that young men ride each day.
We are torn from each other, lost,
some rageful, as we dive down
into our unconscious wounds, awake
to our present reality. There is
no one here in the darkness.
The great storms carry thunder snow.
New rains cause flooding in the west.
There is a sadness at the heart.
The painters will show us colors
and textures of our inner life.
We hope for vibrancy, movement,
our shadows illuminated.
In the distance, musicians
begin to write, sing, chant
of our dark mystery, our protest,
and we honor and embrace
a sadness that will not end soon enough.
There are drums, now, to be played.
We are the strong, grieving, drummers
of our American world. And so I go
downtown early, for a cup of coffee,
5:30 in the morning, and driving,
hear Dave Carlson's band,
Tasmanian Devils, on KRSH radio,
"Roots, Blues, Americana,"

playing a live version of "Not Fade Away,"
as good as it gets rock 'n roll,
powerful before dawn,
the crowd roaring at the end.
And I think I'm going to be all right again,
even with this sadness at the heart of the nation.

WALLY'S FIX-IT SHOP

~ for David Rollison

Sounds, echoes,
remnants, words, driving
with Robert Duncan across
the Golden Gate Bridge, or
Jack Spicer, "Toward some
great Catalina of a dream,"
hills, marshes,
the bay as sanctuary,
early on the sacred nature of
Mount Tam and
a yellow table,
a cowboy clown,
existential thought,
Wally's fix-it shop,
drifting, waking,
books and the news
found there or in
North Beach with
the others, Bob Kaufman
at night, Jack Micheline
sings the streets, Ivan's
famous song, "Heartache"
Barry's mystery pastels,
Jack Gilbert at Spicer's
Poetry as Magic Workshop,
this is the poem,
found, lost, given,
"Often I am permitted

to return to a meadow,"
Duncan wrote and
you wrote "Esther's smile
is a de Kooning brush,"
far and near,
hawks, buzzards, crows,
the poets speak of joy,
art and literature
as a life along with
your wife Sheri dancing

ALCHEMY

a fine morning
a vision of diamonds
light on the cactus

~

now it's afternoon
trees and shadows
ancient fire sun

NEW YORK CITY

there are cities of glass
cities of stone
a long way to go

music studios
and statues
the bridegroom of knowledge

the keeper of bridges
we're heading to Brooklyn
I've told you this before

somewhere in the future
yes, a ceramicist
Dada, 1913,

a coffee cup wrapped in fur
or else
abstract art

all the rock 'n' rollers
Jim Carroll sang it, man
wrote his poems down

DOWN AROUND THE EMBARCADERO

I'm not going I'm not staying
I'm selling my poems
on the corner in my
railroad cap typing out
dreams down around
Fisherman's Wharf
down around
the Embarcadero
every so often
5 bucks a poem
do you see me I see you
the tourists buy my poems
as rough-edged souvenirs
now don't be telling lies
I'm tempted to disappear
east of Santa Fe and
west of nowhere
but I've got a rent controlled
place south of an alley
in Glen Park, San Francisco
I found a bookstore
in the Mission that'll
carry my books for sale
it's morning it's evening
somewhere it's late afternoon
poems for 5 bucks
I've got poems for
a thousand bucks too
you get what you pay for

yet it's all spirit and heart
with a serious nod to
Black Mountain poets
to the Beats and
SF Renaissance poets
if I can just find my way
to the end of the page
the end of the poem
Don Ewell is playing
boogie-woogie piano
a Jelly Roll Morton jazz tune
it's early it's late they
changed the time again
I'm living quiet and easy
worked hard through
and through so
this poem's for my brothers
for my sister and for you
catch me down at the Marina
right near North Beach
out in the Avenues
I'm lost I'm gone
distance intimacy
poetry as truth

ROOFTOP

Stay up all night
from dark till dawn
there was a party earlier
then a rooftop scene
San Rafael mid 70's
sugar cube LSD
you begin to understand
there's magic everywhere
tell Andrea, tell Rand,
tell no one, that's okay
knowledge has a path
your way is one way
I wrote a poem then,
"I stand under the branches
of your voice, dreaming"
and night, on the roof,
lie back on LSD
Alan Watts echoes
philosophy in the mind
who is going where and Eliot
"HURRY UP PLEASE IT'S TIME"
yet let me tell about the stars
we are trails of light
our hands are beacons
no moon new moon
full moon eternity
you are part of the earth
you are a vision of now
flashing by and we hear

from the room just below
Janis Joplin on the stereo
Big Brother and the Holding Company
in a room there is power and sound
in the night air there is imagination
fifty years or so ago
trails of light
leaf decision
trees breathing
Janis and Big Brother
a roof a sky

HIGH FAR MOUNTAINS

this is the way of juniper and pine
think now of eagles at Goat Rock
if you're a fading dream near Taos
or a drifting scene on the Mississippi
tell 'em you're living it through
this road jazz midnight grateful
thankful each and every day
cedar trees in the high far mountains
everywhere the distance comes closer

WATCHING SQUIRRELS

Sick with the flu,
I sit watching squirrels
out the window, on the fence,
and especially when two
squirrels chase each other
round and up and down
the redwood tree. Pure
joy is a subtle thing, like
poetry. Unlike that pesky
death song that keeps on,
just out of earshot.
Meanwhile, Jessica Williams
and Leroy Vinnegar, on piano
and bass, respectively, hold
forth with jazz on the stereo.
This is healing, I think
to myself, a cup of
cinnamon apple tea
warming my hands,
my insides, early Saturday,
sun gleaming into the house.

FIELDS OF ROUGH STONE

What did I wish for
what is the healing mechanism
what then, beauty, what, knowledge
all down the hill road
there were clues of discovery
I lived as a secret agent of dreams
an inner guidance
towards fields of rough stone
I used up the words "oak trees"
still, as in quietly,
I was there under Marin and Sonoma
clouds, rare in summer but there it is
and fires now
changing us as the climate changes
and some fight about core decisions
we are on a small planet
let's say we are in a boat together
no matter color or religion
call out saying
everyone together now
rowing, rowing, let's be at peace
solitude is the middle name
of your grandmother and her
grandmother and we are all going on
I was there near
The City with its luminous bridge
and the sea was with us all

NEXT 78 MILES

Gather your emptiness where you can
and begin again. Let there be silence
and intervals of space between us.
How long have I known you,
didn't we just meet, is winter leaving,
what was her name, that woman in Paris,
after the poetry reading, writing in a cafe,
she said, I will not whisper, I'll tell it straight,
all of this goes away, keep on with me in mind.
I had no plan out beyond where the pavement
turned to dirt and the sign read no roadside
service next 78 miles. This, then, is not
Paris, this is west coast America, gather
your emptiness where you can.

HALF ASLEEP WAKING UP SINGING

it is the darkness
that is waking memories of
the charms of old Marin
we say alabaster and sculptors' stones
we grieve truth and facts and reality
America is a map of possibilities
a trust basin a barometer for health
we are a nation of immigrants it's been said
who are my brothers with colors of various skins
my sisters are Asian African Iranian original
countries or countries of origin give us richness
wealth of history joy of culture and songs of faith
I am an oud player I am a kettle drum man
the sitar has been my teacher I love to say
the name of the musician Ali Ahkbar Khan
he was based in Marin too and then there is
the mountain hello Mount Tamalpais hello
Russian River at the mouth near Jenner
Sonoma County coastal scene
we go on we welcome others and sure
we have our protections our military
our secret intelligence our networks of
information specialists but we also have
our families our cousins everywhere
our aunts and uncles and parents some
in heavenly worlds some right here so
sing out for Tulsa where Cheryl comes from
sing out for librarians in Mendocino and
Birmingham and right here at home

sing out for San Francisco city of trust
The City of dreams at the edge of our nation
bless this house this nation of rivers
and creeks and immigrants having coffee
this blessing goes out to all who are brothers
all who are sisters of the earth and sky
this song travels to all who wake in America
who wake believing in the hope of America
beyond fear and mistrust of others
peace joy wilderness

CITY SHADOW

distinct ease
arrival families
border crossings
death poem
world gone
most of my friends
have no poetry
needs at all
kid says to me "they
won't find
my prints on
the gun"
gets 15 to life
anyway
it's tough times
gang town
why are we alive
caravan on the way
healing rain
everyone needs
an education
in grace
even with no poetry
find yourself
some luck today
nighttime dancing
hiking the canyons
in time we move it's
a blues machine

crows up close
eyes open
mountain lake
city shadow
obscure clarity
old days and today
grace and new trees

MUSIC IN THE RUINS

At the center of the soul
is the heart, even with
darkness all around.
Waking up still night sky
before the light arrives.
Ah, world. I'm listening
to Art Pepper on alto,
his *Smack Up* album,
yeah, he got caught awhile,
did stretches in prison,
that heroin thing, and Connie
says there's still a bunch of
folks showing up at the county
psychiatric crisis unit on meth,
a high percentage really, it's a
bad drug, meth psychosis is
real. Connie says a number
of folks have died in
the community from fentanyl
overdoses, too. Here, the music
is on, jazz before dawn,
and the Bagshaw brothers
are playing somewhere soon,
Jimmy on drums up north,
even if his bass player friend
is moving away, taking his retro
cool Danelectro longhorn bass
with him, and his gal with
her washboard leaving, too.

Jimmy's brother Bernie
has played jazz guitar on
the avenue, the street, in
The City, during the pandemic,
the neighbors happy, with sax
and drums and stand up bass.
I played in a band as a kid
with another Bagshaw brother,
Danny, with John Mann on drums.
Danny a true guitar guy.
I played rhythm or bass, and
Mr. Bagshaw rigged up a
nine-string guitar, doubling
the top three strings for
his kid, Danny, and it sticks
in my mind, one of the coolest
things a parent in old Terra
Linda had done, chiming,
driving, shining nine-string
guitar sounds. Danny on
fire with music, like his
brothers now, these days.
This is not nostalgic, not
lost back in time, knowing,
from where I started this
morning, Art Pepper on
alto sax, man, the heart
at the center of the soul,
drums and jazz guitar right
in there, important, yes,
the heart at the center and

at the end of the poem, too,
knowing the light is
arriving again,
knowing everyone is
headed out and away
on their own train riding
to the spirit world someday.
It's jazz and blues, rock 'n' roll,
and Americana music as we
wane like the moon and
we shine as we fade.
There's music in the ruins
and we know where
the heart resides.

NIGHTHAWK

if all suffering
was over

then America
rainy day jacket

sustenance
or green trees

no one owns the sky yet
wait here

I've set these words down carefully

medicine tincture
collage art

nighthawk dedication and
anybody can speak

want not want say need

now read the poem
another way

let your body dream
count on this

truth serum

POETICS # 1

it was on the verge of the desert
                    sublime sense

        with death

                is all ridiculous

waking and crises

            (daisies)

                    the rock rose is native to California

POETICS # 2

the old cellist
comes to grieve
his mind is going
wild lilac

the Dry Mountains
in sight of the Inyo Mountains

language as the water

inlet

knife blade

dusk

one hundred miles from Alturas
double hummingbird and the early work

IN A WILD PLACE

~ written with Elizabeth C. Herron

In a wild place
anything is possible.
Dreams come home.
Deer at the edge of meadow
graze the light,
breath to earth. Between us,
something beginning.
The forest grows dark with waiting.
A slow stampede of rain
reaches ground.

COLORS

skylight midnight jet black
Elizabeth's poems over time
west county news and trailside
truths are like stars
O visible
in everyone's awakening mind
elegant river stones
how do we all say goodbye
change in the air winter's coming
this is not the end I'm nearby
candy apple red and tangerine

WAKE EARLY

"Who digs Los Angeles IS Los Angeles"
– Allen Ginsberg

wake early
night undone

dark city
modern thought

use 'ubiquitous'
in a poem

after all the mirrors
let's go to L.A. then

in surprise
with anonymity

Lincoln Boulevard
into town

she's ready to go
she's not waiting

ocean ocean
earth and sea

I told you about that time
I sensed your wildness your vibrancy

BOBCAT COYOTE RAVENS

we have waited for the rain
we live with afternoon winds
this is the road at dusk
the time when the earth changes
everyone is here
even bobcat coyote ravens
legends of the sky and mountains
this world or the spirit world
forgotten waylaid lamented
found and found again

HOLLY'S IDEA / A WORD FOR THE YEAR

didn't get it done
did get it done
words on the way

serendipity
intuition
knowledge all along

bought time
brought flowers
left town

her essence rhymes
she's in sync
a graceful exit too

way out west
Sonny Rollins again
of course it depends

Lily's near Yellow Springs
we danced across fire
hippies round here

I'll find my way
graves and graves
saxophone valley

I have half a mind
to tell the story as
echo crystal

horned toad
creosote bush
ancient energy

the newness of you

JANA AND ALAN WATTS' HOUSEBOAT

Jana Watts trips on acid
Sausalito houseboat gentle waves
earlier Gary Snyder / Allen Ginsberg reading

Palace Of Fine Arts San Francisco August 1974
seventeen years old just got done playing baseball
high school ball in Marin and going on a wilderness

trip with Steven Foster and Dr. Tom Pinkson
Steven brings me along to the poetry reading
it's a benefit for the Alan Watts Philosophical Society

Watts died the year before and G. Sandman
on our wilderness trip to Yosemite also
lived on the boat a big ferry the Vallejo

Sandman the secretary of the Watts Society
there's Jana on LSD in white robes asks G.
did you know Alan oh Alan would have loved you

there's *papier-mâché* art therapy animals
hanging from the ceiling we're all smoking hash
a guy's talking about the artist Jean Varda

Varda used to sit right there wicker chair
so he could get high and simply turn
around and fall into the daybed

earlier Snyder sitting cross-legged Zen prayer beads
after years studying in Japan
Gary's learned outdoors quick-witted writings

Ginsberg big beard New York City voice
cross-legged also on pillows on the floor on stage
Ginsberg leads everyone with harmonium

a 25-minute Om we're all chanting together
there's hope still just after the end of the sixties
there's elegance mysticism

I'm seventeen and realize right away or realize over time
realize in a flash of haze and hash and San Francisco Bay
there's idyllic poetry there's music everywhere

Jana Watts is swirling seeing dancing in her flowing robes
houseboat houseboat dreams of the day wisdom in breath
Ginsberg's long lines of poetry last forever Snyder's prayers

everyone chanting then and even today fifty years later
there's Mount Tam shining earth to sky to mind now
oh ah Om okay

CHRISTMAS IN COPENHAGEN

many of the jazz players
in the 1960's left for Paris
or Copenhagen while
the music still thrived
on the continent of dreams
and there was ostensibly
less racism against Blacks
compared to here in the States –
I'm thinking of Dexter Gordon
and others, thinking of you with
your intimations of mortality
your judicial sense of how
the deck is now stacked
against progressive liberalism
the pendulum swinging
back and forth or spinning
round and round in your town
wherever you are celebrating
say Christmas in Copenhagen
or take Jack Gilbert's famous
miniature of a poem, Jack said
he liked to make mountains
out of molehills, packing the
power in, tight, so a poem
expands in the mind, his poem
"Alone On Christmas Eve In Japan,"
looking out over a graveyard,
or the way Lorca wrote
about *duende*, a sense

of the presence of death, and
indeed, Franco had the poet
killed in Spain, while Kenneth
Patchen, in chronic pain, wrote
"O, the poets with death on their
tongues shall come to address
you," and we are here, moving
in our great journey toward each
other, toward the next world, too,
and they are celebrating soon,
Christmas in Copenhagen
with jazz on the turntable,
snow fields and lamps lit,
with poems beginning in
the long winter night of stars.

BLUE GRAY CITY

O, I have to dismantle some of my poems
now
to see the essence of things

    blue gray sky
    San Francisco at 6th and
    Clement walking, walking

    let's go to the bookstore study
    the psyche
    find a novel

when your emptiness
is gone

THE ETERNAL BIRD

I am searching for the luminous
this redwood and that fir resiliency
her heartache was made of years
sleeping alone in the forest drifting
from woods to rivers
he spied the eternal bird

home grown apples out of
Sebastopol and your ruby red intimacy
this is her desire taken to known
rest amid mountains just there
there is where we find the gold
long gone our California riverbed any
gems are inside as infinity

51

LISTENING TO DUKE ELLINGTON
AND JOHN COLTRANE

rhythmic piano
and wild saxophone
you were swingin' before
you were all about bop and
post bop and free jazz too
it seems the moon is ours
early before dawn where
live oaks stand and
all I can say listening is
I'm dreaming again
I hope you're dreaming too
when I said goodbye
I didn't know about endings
really and beginning again
Duke Ellington taught us
teaches us and ol' John Coltrane
who never got old sings about
a love supreme and why not
I'm leaving someday and bless
your heart you're leaving too
so let's take those songs in mind
the rhythms in time let's say
we've got Duke with Coltrane's
classic quartet heading home
closer to the end than the beginning
nothing much to say and saying
it anyway I'm stealing lines from
my own poems like George Oppen
did and I'll take sublime cool jazz

later today low key vibrant Zoot Sims
I'll tell my friends to dig in for
the long haul to roll with the changes
the maps are gone it's your own road now
I'm off in the woods I'm over at the lake
oh yeah I'm down by the river in shade
I'm deep in the desert canyon where
truth is silence where the wind is song
rocks and stones tell us stories
of our good fortune didn't I see you
yesterday you were dreaming awake
talking poetry and magic and the news
about the pandemic blues I heard
Shakey Horton blowing harp on the radio
and Hound Dog Taylor on slide guitar
driving driving then waking up
this morning on my birthday
I'm counting backwards in years
I'm getting younger in spirit it seems
tricking myself best I can ha that's the way
with Duke Ellington and John Coltrane
groovin' and movin' and cruising on down

WIND FROM THE MOUNTAINS OUT TO THE COAST

the wind
travels fierce
at twilight

    the shadow lands
        storms without warning

hidden, eyes,
weeping,
a way in

hands
hold energy

    enlightenment
        shining

huge sky
darkens

THE RAINY SEASON

People sit on couches
waiting for wisdom to arrive.
Still, lying politicians lie.
In the near dark winter
evening, a single lamp.
Listening to Little Feat
on the stereo loud, loud.
"I've been down, but not
like this before." Thinking,
I'm not down, I'm dancing
in the living room. The country
in trouble, the earth struggling,
Little Feat, loud. All my
friends tell it straight.
After the song, hearing
the rain again. The first
rainy season in years.
Maybe the drought is over,
maybe the politicians
will get real.
Waiting for the truth to
return to America. Time
for some west coast jazz
in the rain soaked world.

GOING TO THE SAN FRANCISCO GIANTS
GAME WITH LAWRENCE FERLINGHETTI

Death, you got him,
the oldest poet, at 101,
San Francisco man,
a dreamer, a painter,
but not really, Mr. Death.
Lawrence lives on in books
& paintings such as "Sun Boat # 2,"
a favorite. Ferlinghetti always
spoke out against injustice,
risked the law publishing
Ginsberg's "Howl,"
on trial for obscenity, 1950's,
and in the late 90's,
I hung out with Lawrence often,
at Susie's ranch near Petaluma.
We'd talk of poetry and art,
Kenneth Patchen's picture poems
and hand-painted books, and
back when I smoked a little pot,
we'd smoke a little pot, laughing,
glassy-eyed in West Marin, really,
among the oaks and stone boulders.
Lawrence with his creaky voice,
me saying how his "pennycandystore
beyond the El" let me imagine a new
world at fifteen. Lawrence liked hanging
out with Caz. "She's real," Lawrence said.

Then the time I went to a Giants baseball game
sitting in the stands with Lawrence,
box seats above the home team dugout.
Lawrence and I talking about
the Giants' second baseman
back in the 60's, Tito Fuentes.
Lawrence had written about Tito in
his poem "Baseball Canto."
Lawrence died yesterday at 101,
his City Lights Bookstore in SF still going,
literally the first paperback bookstore
in America, where Connie likes to sit
upstairs in the Poetry Room, in that
rickety old "poet's chair," a rocker.
Lawrence was such a great spirit
when he was a man, death
has just whisked him away
to be a great spirit in the spirit land.
Lawrence Ferlinghetti
made The City a literary place, with
all the others, he gave voice to joy,
gave voice to political resistance,
gave voice to the heart of America.
Just ten years ago Lawrence recited
poems from memory, age 91, at a reading
with Gary Snyder in North Beach, and yes,
we got lucky, all of us, having Lawrence around,
oh, a good long time.

CANYONS

you must live a spiritual life
I heard myself say
in a poem not to be published
the earth is our only hope
going forward
a crystal in the window
the kind you found in the desert
years ago when Steven was alive
and we knew the names of canyons
a ways away poems in the mind
old days of political news
lawn chairs in the afternoon
sun as a teacher moon as witness
these are the tears of a nation
humbled by our simple house
where a deep shadow moves
and here the poem says enough
make a new way
for yourself and with your friends
this overarching song
this loss and grief
reclaim your wilderness heart make
your chant of power
smoky quartz, chalcedony
fire opal, turquoise healing stone
I will keep your secret music awake
with the traveling ravens and the
bold red-tailed hawks
near us even now

IN CALIFORNIA

In California, many complain of
the rain if it goes on too long.
Which is strange, given these
years of astonishing drought.
Some women dream of art,
lithographs, etchings that burnish
hidden paths of the mind. Some
women fear for their children's
future, the earth in crisis, a planet
experiencing trauma. We don't
know if it's in the cards for this
planet to survive. We know we
ourselves must die. Oh fate,
oh long trail of destiny, hold
us true. I know a bit about grief,
I talk of joy and magic and
rain in the trees, occasionally hail,
a ton of snow in Tahoe
or east of the Sierras in
Mammoth. The poem itself
is a sculpture, a collage,
a way of life, a resonance,
a following along with subtle
sounds, the coast nearby, and the
highway, with women,
beautiful and sad and hopeful,
seeking to trust the depths,
seeking to believe in the road.

APRICOT

~ for Juliet

deer   window

                    nine a.m.

grasses

        stars return

gone
    lost
the body as reservoir

                            old silver mines

      a phrase carried in the mind

                the pond in autumn

apricot, ghost town,
the thieves of winter

alabaster, a sculptor's stone

the camera as music

cold moon and earth
and silence in the room

photogravure, shadow box, pinhole

the brown recluse spider

waterways

the nature of dance
words eclipsed in fields

of white

HEROIN OPIOID BLUES

American towns lost
in sorrow and pain
has been actualized
heroin and opioids
have taken over lives
pain is real in the body
and the mind here
in America no song
or poem touches this
fact of how the sorrow
has entered our nation
lost hope ghost memory
strength buried along
with so many overdose
victims in so many places
heroin opioid blues
news from the towns
humans without hope
let's go for harm reduction
comprehensive treatment
can't kill Medicaid without
harming humans
pain management man
people in darkness
people moving back
towards the light
sun healing
moon healing
songs of the opioid epidemic

poems about people in pain
sun healing
moon healing
heroin opioid blues

THE DISTANCE BETWEEN LOVE
AND FRESNO

Without a poem,
words drift away.
Talk suffices at night.
Consciously choosing
not to argue with loved
ones. The wood stove
hot, door open awhile,
cabin life, stark forest,
creating joy with art,
which is magic. Now
to make it through dark
rainy cold months, while
a poet friend says she's
concerned she has no
project. We discuss fallow
times, moving away, to
a place where nothing
happens except silence
enters in, breath slows,
dreams return. This is
the morning of storms.
This is a winter of trust.
There are a few places in
nature where certain fireflies
mate and the light becomes
synchronized, attuned and
in many ways, the light of
this world, now, today,

where you are, is healing.
The light is everything.

HEAVY METAL / LIVE AT THE PHOENIX

kids wait outside for their lives
to unfurl with music
metal truths darken the entrance way

at the Hotel Petaluma
folks who didn't get rich listen
to echoes and memories

the poet Gene Ruggles
died at the hotel
drinking and writing

chasing
the water lily
and the music at the Phoenix Theater begins

THE LONG JAM

I've forgotten everything
about Zen masters
I sit listening to a jazz player
not well-known but excellent
adept
B.G. (Bunky Green)
it is summer in the west
next I lean in early
and play along with long jams
by Country Joe & The Fish
Fillmore Auditorium 1969
Jack Casady on bass
the poems are nearly done
three new books written
a California trilogy
now until the end
notes and wanderings
might write like the old
mountain poets
a poem now and again
might write a journal
call it "Cabin Studies"
leave for the ocean
leave with friends
arrive and jam

JUKEBOX NEW YEAR

death shadow blues
old news gone year
discard everything
sing again
off-tune even
this way to everywhere
what say you
call in silence
bottle tops
restoration redemption
I have told you and told you
now you've done it
how young everyone looks
dictatorial aspirations all
around the world
who works for ammunition companies
tremendous lines of poetry say
Theodore Roethke far northwest
Robert Creeley out of breath
succinct balance
she said
wet world rain
Fred Neil singing
then off to work with dolphins
a time of folksingers
lost mind
dedicated to earth
go on get back before dark
you've seen the stars

moon with Venus
trust parallel
Randy's spent his life
as a professor of Chemistry
Gary's on the keyboards now
Claude's playing electric bass
when he's not painting wild
here's where the world takes us
all women know revolution
in their body mind spirit
tell no lies the country's
off track with lies
Andrea dances listens in
Sheila keeps a sketchbook
I write poems distant canyons
shenanigans
wood and wire ladder
to navigate the waterfall
say hello to Janice
John's metal sculptures out
of Baton Rouge
again, FDR said, "I hate war"
here we are walking together
Turner's "Morning With Sea Monsters"
fog early California
light breaks through in the afternoon

MAPS

trains across the Mojave
what if poems are maps of the soul
writing, disappearance, a myth all along

ACKNOWLDEGMENTS

Many thanks to Mae Blackmore, Caz, Mary Kane,
Jim Morgan, and Connie Von Arx.

Thanks to the editors of the publications where versions of
the following poems were published in print or online:

"Enter the Poem Dreaming" and "Holly's Idea / A Word
for the Year" were published in *100subtexts* magazine.

"Next 78 Miles," "Colors," and "Bobcat Coyote Ravens"
were first published in the chapbook *Next 78 Miles* from
Littoral Press, 2020.

"Half Asleep Waking Up Singing" was published in
Nostos: Poetry, Fiction and Art.

"Poetics # 1" was published in *Try* magazine.

"Poetics # 2" and '"Heavy Metal / Live at the Phoenix"
were published in *Local Nomad / A Journal of the Arts*.

"In a Wild Place" first appeared as a broadside, designed
and printed by Gregg Loew, for a poetry reading by Jack
Crimmins and Elizabeth C. Herron, at Garbo's Restaurant
and Bar, Guerneville, California, 1980. Elizabeth and I have
collaborated ever since, though this is the only poem we've
written together. Elizabeth's poems and books are elegant,
earth-driven.

"Apricot" first appeared as a folded letterpress broadside
published by Littoral Press, 2007, and later featured in

Visual Poetry: Treasures of the Book Club Library, The Book Club of California Keepsake for 2023 by Elizabeth Newsom.

"Apricot" is for photographer Juliet van Otteren.

"Maps" first appeared as a letterpress broadside, designed and printed by Hilary Smith at the San Francisco Center for the Book, 2024.

The poem "Holly's Idea / A Word for the Year" was inspired by Holly Barker Lee.

"Down Around the Embarcadero" first appeared as a spoken word poem, with music by Olds Sleeper, on "Connections 8: Music & Poetry" in benefit of KRCB-FM, Sonoma County's National Public Radio station. Thanks to Olds Sleeper, Doug Jayne, and Max Allen.

Jack Casady (Jefferson Airplane, Hot Tuna) played electric bass with Country Joe & The Fish at the live gig and on the album *Country Joe & The Fish and Friends: Live! Fillmore West 1969.*

The Allen Ginsberg quote used as an epigraph for "Wake Early" is from Ginsberg's "Footnote to Howl."

Please note that I'm aware that there's likely great love in Fresno, California. I like the title of the poem nonetheless.

Thanks to all my friends who sometimes show up in my poems, or are hidden in my poems; you know who you are.

Jack Crimmins is the author of *Kit Fox Blues*, *The Rust Life*, *Dancing in the Sun Room*, and *The Edge of Rain*. He has worked for many years as a licensed psychotherapist and lives in Sonoma County, California.

www.ingramcontent.com/pod-product-compliance
Lightning Source LLC
Chambersburg PA
CBHW021706150626
46549CB00016B/1121